Tails

written by
Marcia Vaughan

illustrated by
Lyn McMurdie

BOOKSHELF

Whose tail is long?

Whose tail is curly?

Whose tail is short?

Whose tail is furry?

Whose tail is feathered?

Whose tail is stumpy?

Whose tail is scaly?

Whose tail is bumpy?

Whose tail is pointed?

Whose tail is flat?

Whose tail is prickly?

Whose tail is fat?

Whose tail is striped?

Whose tail is like a ball?

Who doesn't have a tail at all?